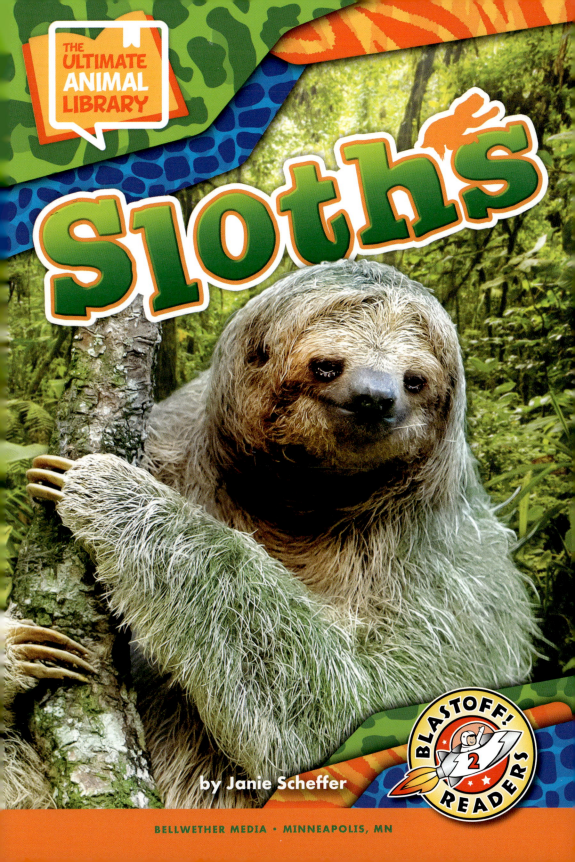

Sloths

THE ULTIMATE ANIMAL LIBRARY

by Janie Scheffer

BLASTOFF! READERS 2

BELLWETHER MEDIA • MINNEAPOLIS, MN

Blastoff! Readers are carefully developed by literacy experts to build reading stamina and move students toward fluency by combining standards-based content with developmentally appropriate text.

LEVELS

Level 1 provides the most support through repetition of high-frequency words, light text, predictable sentence patterns, and strong visual support.

Level 2 offers early readers a bit more challenge through varied sentences, increased text load, and text-supportive special features.

Level 3 advances early-fluent readers toward fluency through increased text load, less reliance on photos, advancing concepts, longer sentences, and more complex special features.

★ Blastoff! Universe

Reading Level

Grade K

Grades 1–3

Grade 4

This edition first published in 2026 by Bellwether Media, Inc.

No part of this publication may be reproduced in whole or in part without written permission of the publisher. For information regarding permission, write to Bellwether Media, Inc., Attention: Permissions Department, 3500 American Blvd West, Suite 190, Bloomington, MN 55431.

Library of Congress Cataloging-in-Publication Data

LC record for Sloths available at: https://lccn.loc.gov/2025003952

Text copyright © 2026 by Bellwether Media, Inc. BLASTOFF! READERS and associated logos are trademarks and/or registered trademarks of Bellwether Media, Inc. Bellwether Media is a division of FlutterBee Education Group.

Editor: Elizabeth Neuenfeldt   Series Designer: Veah Demmin

Printed in the United States of America, North Mankato, MN.

Table of Contents

What Are Sloths?	4
Slow Days	12
Growing Up	18
Glossary	22
To Learn More	23
Index	24

What Are Sloths?

Sloths are the slowest **mammals** on Earth. There are two-toed and three-toed sloths. They all live in Central America and South America.

Brown-throated Sloth Report

Range

range = 🟩

Status in the Wild

✓ ✓ ✓ ✓ ✓ ✓ ✓ ✗

least concern

Habitat

rain forests

5

Sloths have grayish-brown **coats**. They look green because **algae** grow on them. Their colors help them hide from **predators**.

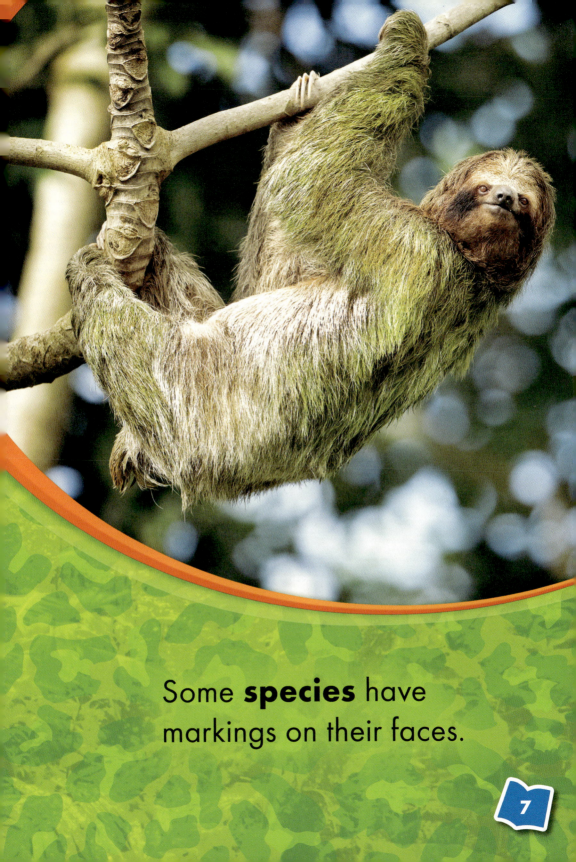

Some **species** have markings on their faces.

claws

Sloths have long, sharp claws. Some species have two claws on their front feet. Others have three claws.

Claws help sloths hang from trees.

Sloths have long front legs. Their front legs are strong. They help sloths climb and swim.

Their back legs are shorter.

Slow Days

Sloths live alone in **rain forests**. They rest and eat in trees.

They sleep up to 20 hours a day. They are mostly **nocturnal**.

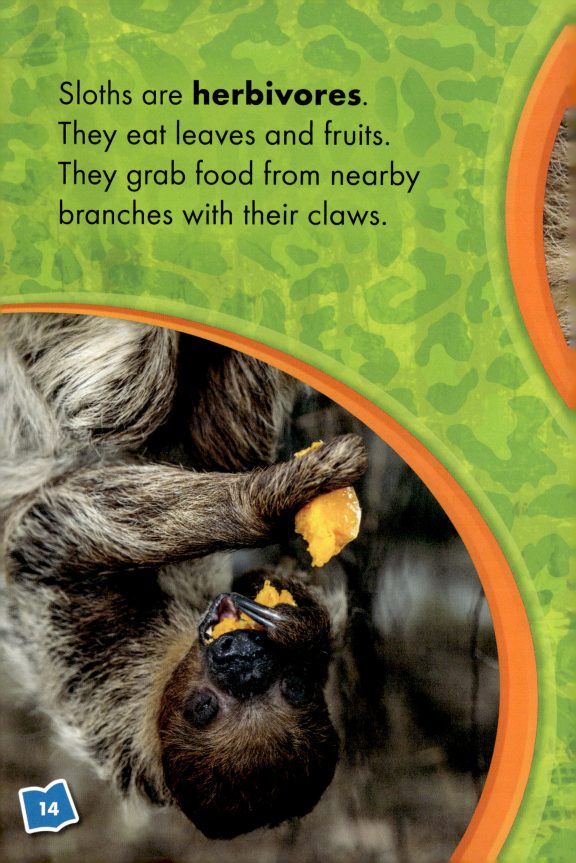

Sloths are **herbivores**. They eat leaves and fruits. They grab food from nearby branches with their claws.

Leaves give sloths most of the water they need.

Sloths eat and **digest** food slowly. Their stomachs are usually full. It can take them a week to digest a meal.

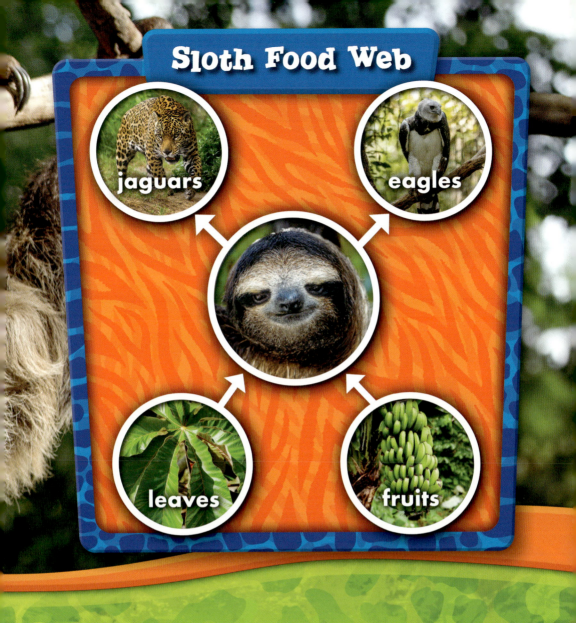

This helps explain their low **energy**!

Growing Up

Sloths **mate** in trees. Mothers give birth to one baby sloth at a time.

Baby sloths tightly hold onto their mothers.

baby sloth

Baby sloths stay with their mothers for up to two years. Then they live on their own.

Sloths can live for many years!

Life of a Sloth

Name of Babies

 baby sloths

Number of Babies

 1

Time Spent with Mom

up to two years

Life Span

 30 to 40 years

Glossary

algae—plants and plantlike living things; most kinds of algae grow in water.

coats—the fur or hair covering some animals

digest—to break down food

energy—the power to move and do things

herbivores—animals that only eat plants

mammals—warm-blooded animals that have backbones and feed their young milk

mate—to join together to have babies

nocturnal—active at night

predators—animals that hunt other animals for food

rain forests—thick, green forests that receive a lot of rain

species—kinds of an animal

To Learn More

AT THE LIBRARY

Chang, Kirsten. *Baby Monkey or Baby Sloth?* Minneapolis, Minn.: Bellwether Media, 2026.

Hansen, Amy. *Curious about Sloths.* Mankato, Minn.: Amicus, 2023.

Rocco, Hayley. *Hello, I'm a Sloth.* New York, N.Y.: G.P. Putnam's Sons, 2024.

ON THE WEB

FACTSURFER

Factsurfer.com gives you a safe, fun way to find more information.

1. Go to www.factsurfer.com.

2. Enter "sloths" into the search box and click.

3. Select your book cover to see a list of related content.

Index

algae, 6
baby, 18, 20
Central America, 4
claws, 8, 9, 14
climb, 10
coats, 6
colors, 6
digest, 16
energy, 17
food, 14, 15, 16, 17
herbivores, 14
hide, 6
legs, 10
life of a sloth, 21
mammals, 4
markings, 7
mate, 18
mothers, 18, 20
nocturnal, 13
predators, 6

rain forests, 12
range, 4, 5
sleep, 13
South America, 4
species, 7, 8
spot a sloth, 11
status, 5
swim, 10
three-toed sloths, 4
trees, 9, 12, 18
two-toed sloths, 4
water, 15

The images in this book are reproduced through the courtesy of: Milan Zygmunt, cover (sloth); Horia Bogdan, cover background, interior background; Airin.dizain, cover (sloth icon); Passakorn, pp. 3, 23; Milan, pp. 4, 6, 7; Diego Grandi, p. 8; dam, pp. 9, 21; Suzi Eszterhas/ Minden Pictures, p. 10; GERARD, pp. 10-11; Lukas, p. 11; SPARKLINGTRAVEL, p. 12; victor, p. 13; jonaldopc, p. 14; Ivan Kuzmin, p. 15; nattanan726, pp. 16-17; christian vinces, p. 17 (jaguars); Piotr Krzeslak, p. 17 (fruits); Murilo, p. 17 (eagles); juerginho, p. 17 (leaves); Wirestock, p. 17 (sloth); lemalfaiteur, p. 18; Audrey, pp. 18-19; Harry Collins, p. 20.